PANDAS

BY VALERIE BODDEN

W
FRANKLIN WATTS
LONDON•SYDNEY

D0230015

RENFREWSHIRE COUNCIL	
186473721	
Bertrams	08/07/2013
599.789	£11.99
CEN	

First published in the UK in 2013 by
Franklin Watts
338 Euston Road
London NW1 3BH

Franklin Watts Australia
Level 17/207 Kent Street
Sydney NSW 2000

First published by Creative Education,
an imprint of the Creative Company
Copyright © 2013 Creative Education
International copyright reserved in all countries.
No part of this book may be reproduced in any
form without written permission from the publisher.

All rights reserved.

ISBN 978 1 4451 1925 0
Dewey number: 599.7'89

A CIP catalogue record for this book is
available from the British Library.

Printed in China

Franklin Watts is a division of Hachette
Children's Books, an Hachette UK company
www.hachette.co.uk

Design and production by The Design Lab
Art direction by Rita Marshall

Photographs by 123rf (Alexander Muntean), Alamy
(Danita Delimont), Dreamstime (Isselee, Liumangtiger,
Ron Sumners), Getty Images (Nada Pecnik, Keren
Su), National Geographic (KATHERINE FENG/
MINDEN PICTURES), Shutterstock (Hung Chung Chih,
iBird, Juhku, worldswildlifewonders), SuperStock
(Minden Pictures)

CONTENTS

What are pandas?

A panda is a member of the bear family. All bears are **mammals**. Pandas are an **endangered** animal. There are only about 1,600 pandas living in the wild today. People have moved into areas where pandas like to live so there is not enough space or food for more pandas to survive.

This wild panda lives in a forest in China.

mammal an animal that drinks milk from its mother when it is a baby.
endangered an animal of which there are only a small number left on Earth.

Panda facts

Pandas have thick black and white fur. They have sharp claws and very strong jaws. Their front paws have an extra bone and a pad that looks like a thumb. This 'thumb' helps a panda to hold its food when it is eating.

A panda's strong claws and teeth help it to eat woody food.

Small bears

The biggest pandas are about 1.8 metres long. They can weigh up to 130 kilogrammes. Male pandas are usually bigger than females. But pandas are also one of the smallest kinds of bear in the world. They are much smaller than polar or grizzly bears.

Pandas can swim well and enjoy being in the water.

Where pandas live

Wild pandas only live in **bamboo** forests in the middle of China. China is a large country on the **continent** of Asia. The bamboo grows on cool, rainy or snowy **mountains**.

A panda's thick fur keeps it warm in snowy weather.

bamboo a type of tall grass with a tough stem and leaves.
continent one of Earth's seven big pieces of land.
mountains very big hills made of rock.

Panda food

Bamboo is one of the fastest-growing plants in the world.

Pandas eat bamboo. Bamboo is a kind of grass that looks like a very thin tree. It has leaves and a thick, hollow stem. Pandas can eat more than 36 kilogrammes of bamboo every day! Pandas will sometimes eat flowers, rats and other **rodents**, too.

rodent small animals such as rabbits and mice that have sharp front teeth.

New pandas

A female panda will give birth to one or two **cubs** in a **den**. Newborn cubs are tiny – they weigh less than a tube of toothpaste! Usually only one of the cubs will survive. Young pandas are **prey** for leopards and wild dogs. A cub will stay with its mother until it is about two years old. Pandas can live for up to 20 years in the wild.

*Female pandas raise their cubs
without any help from the male.*

cubs baby bears.
den a home that is hidden, like a cave.
prey animals that are eaten by other animals.

Panda life

Adult pandas live alone. They spend 12 hours every day eating bamboo. They sometimes eat sitting up with their back against a tree. Pandas do not move very far or very quickly, but they can climb trees. Pandas also spend a lot of their time sleeping. Unlike most other types of bear, pandas don't **hibernate** in the winter.

Pandas enjoy climbing trees – and sleeping!

hibernate when an animal goes to sleep for the winter, usually in an underground den.

Gentle pandas

Pandas are quite shy, gentle animals. They don't usually attack people or other animals, but they will defend themselves if they are attacked. Young pandas will sometimes roll and play together on the ground. Pandas are generally quiet, but they can bark, growl and squeal.

Young pandas like to play and wrestle with each other.

Pandas and people

Not many people have seen pandas in the wild. But some people study them at **research centres** in China. Some pandas also live in zoos around the world. It can be fun to see these furry bears up close!

This panda is playing in an old tyre at a research centre in China.

research centres places where people study something, such as an animal, to learn more about it.

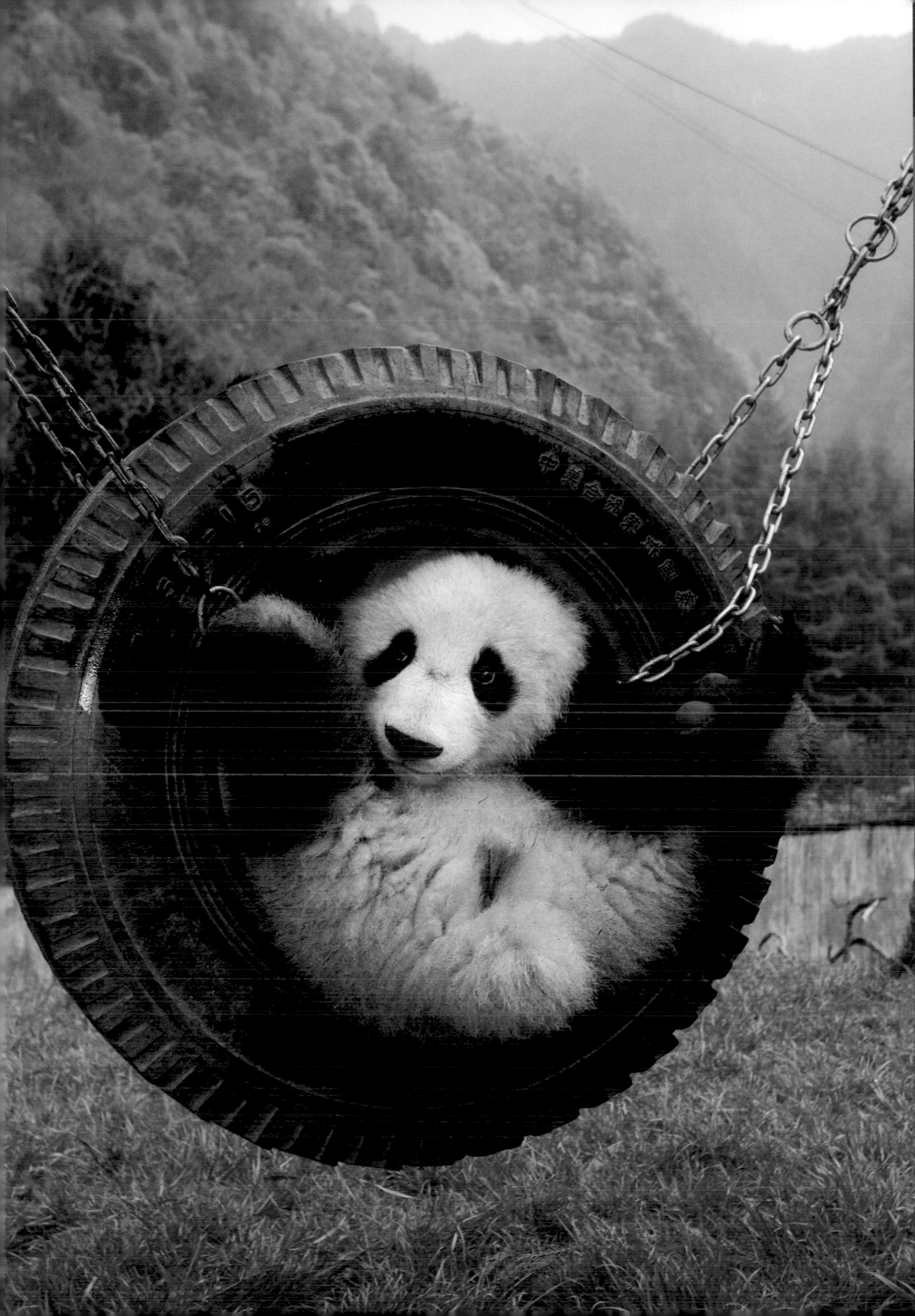

A panda story

Why are pandas black and white? A story from China says that pandas used to be all white. Then one day, a little girl saved a panda cub from a leopard. But the girl died when the leopard attacked her. The pandas were so sad that they pawed the ground and cried. They wiped their eyes with their muddy paws and hugged each other. The mud from their paws left black marks. Pandas have had black and white fur ever since.

Useful information

Read More

Saving Wildlife: Mountain Animals by Sonya Newland
(Franklin Watts, 2010)

Eco Alert: Saving Wildlife by Rebecca Hunter (Franklin Watts, 2010)

Websites

http://kids.nationalgeographic.com/kids/animals/creaturefeature/panda/
This site has panda facts, pictures and videos.

http://gowild.wwf.org.uk/asia
This site has factfiles, games and a panda mask-making activity.

http://www.sandiegozoo.org/pandacam/index.html
This site has a live video of pandas at the San Diego Zoo in
California.

Every effort has been made by the Publishers to ensure that these websites are suitable
for children, that they are of the highest educational value and that they contain no
inappropriate or offensive material. However, because of the nature of the Internet, it is
impossible to guarantee that the contents of these sites will not be altered. We strongly
advise that Internet access is supervised by a responsible adult.

Index